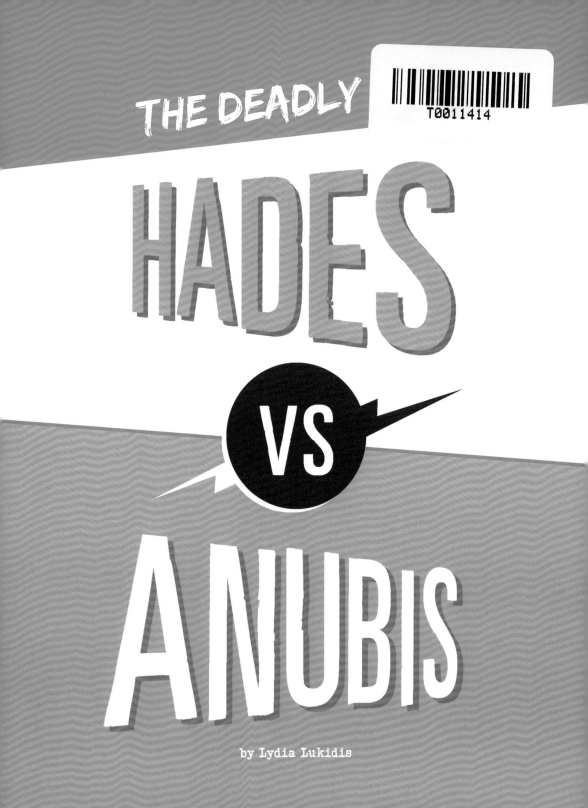

THE DEADLY

HADES

VS

ANUBIS

by Lydia Lukidis

CAPSTONE PRESS
a capstone imprint

T0011414

Published by Capstone Press, an imprint of Capstone.
1710 Roe Crest Drive, North Mankato, Minnesota 56003
capstonepub.com

Library of Congress Cataloging-in-Publication Data is available
on the Library of Congress website
ISBN: 9781669016342 (hardcover)
ISBN: 9781669016298 (paperback)
ISBN: 9781669016304 (ebook PDF)

Summary:
Get ready for a battle to rule the underworld! The Greek god Hades is the king of
the underworld and has power over the souls of the dead. But the Egyptian god
Anubis also claims to rule the underworld and protect people's souls. If these two
ancient gods battled it out one-on-one, who would come out on top?

Editorial Credits
Editor: Aaron Sautter; Designer: Bobbie Nuytten; Media Researcher: Rebekah
Hubstenberger; Production Specialist: Whitney Schaefer

Image Credits
Alamy: Charles Walker Collection, 11, Chronicle, 25, mauritius images GmbH, 4,
28, The Picture Art Collection, 15; Dreamstime: Maryzu, 13 (top); Getty Images:
duncan1890, 19, Hulton Archive, 17, 20, 21, iStock/NSA Digital Archive, 27,
mikroman6, 24, iStock/porpeller, 13 (bottom), iStock/sharifphoto, 8, ZU_09, 6; The
Metropolitan Museum of Art: Gift of Mrs. Myron C. Taylor, 1938, cover (bottom
left); Shutterstock: erichon, 23, InksyndromeArtwork, 5, 29, Konstantin Lazarev,
cover (top right), Malysh Falko, 9, matrioshka, 16, rudall30, 7

All internet sites appearing in back matter were available and accurate when this
book was sent to press.

Printed and bound in China. PO5379

TABLE OF CONTENTS

Words in **bold** are in the glossary.

KINGS OF THE UNDERWORLD

GRRRR! HOWOOOO!

Cerberus, the three-headed dog, guards the entrance to the underworld. He protects his master, Hades.

Hades is the god of the dead in ancient Greek myths. He's a loner king who lives in the dark and gloomy underworld. But make no mistake. Although Hades isn't an Olympian, he's an important and powerful god.

Hades

Suddenly, another god of the dead pops out of the shadows. Anubis is the god of the ancient Egyptian underworld. He has the body of a man and the head of a black jackal. His main job is to protect the dead. Anubis is one of the most popular Egyptian gods.

Who is more powerful? Who has more abilities? Which of these gods of the dead will be the victor? They'll have to battle it out to see who wins!

Anubis

HOW DID THEY GET HERE?

Hades' birth story isn't exactly normal. He was the first son of the Greek **Titans** Cronus and Rhea. They ruled the ancient world. They had several children. But one day an **oracle** warned Cronus that one of his sons would defeat him.

What did Cronus do? He swallowed his first five children: Hades, Hestia, Demeter, Hera, and Poseidon. Rhea decided that wouldn't happen to their youngest child, Zeus. She hid Zeus away to keep him safe. Meanwhile, Hades and his siblings remained in Cronus's belly for many years.

When Zeus grew up, he gave Cronus a potion that made him throw up. Then, PLOP! Hades popped out along with his siblings, fully grown.

Rhea tricked Cronus into swallowing a stone instead of the baby Zeus.

Three Powerful Brothers

Once Cronus's children were freed, the Olympians fought and defeated the Titans. They locked the Titans away in the depths of the underworld. Afterward, Hades, Zeus, and Poseidon randomly chose where they would rule. Zeus became the ruler of the gods and the sky. Poseidon became king of the sea. And Hades became the god of the underworld.

There are a few different stories about Anubis's origin. In earlier times, people believed he was the son of Ra and Hesat. Ra was the king of all gods and the sun. Hesat was a goddess in the form of a cow.

At that point, Anubis was the only god of the dead. But later, Osiris took over the position in Egyptian myths. Anubis then became the son of Osiris instead.

Statue of Anubis

According to one famous tale, Osiris was married to Isis. But one day, the goddess Nephthys fell in love with Osiris. Together, they had a baby named Anubis.

But Nephthys then abandoned Anubis. She was afraid her husband would find out about the child and be angry. Isis then found Anubis and adopted him as her own.

Osiris and Isis

TWO MIGHTY GODS

Make way for Hades! As god of the dead and king of the underworld, Hades is very powerful. His leadership and confidence give him a strong and commanding presence. What he says goes.

Unfortunately, Hades often gets a bad reputation. He might be the god of the dead, but he's not cruel. Hades doesn't spend his time torturing people. Instead, he serves and defends the rights of the dead.

Paradise and Punishment

In Greek mythology, every soul gets sent to the underworld. One part is a paradise to reward great heroes and demigods. But if people committed crimes or offended the gods, they'd be sent to Tartarus. It was a dark and scary place of punishment. Many monsters like the Cyclops lived there.

Hades has a soft side too. When Orpheus's wife died, he journeyed to the underworld to get her back. Orpheus played beautiful music for Hades that warmed his heart. Hades decided to let Orpheus take his wife back to the world of the living.

But there was one condition—both were forbidden to look back. Unfortunately, as they saw the sun again, Orpheus turned back to look at his wife. In that moment, she disappeared.

Orpheus lost his wife, Eurydice, forever after looking back as they left the underworld.

Anubis is similar to Hades. He's the Egyptian god of the underworld. He also has complete power and authority over the dead.

Not all Egyptian souls are allowed into the underworld. Anubis stands for justice and decides who can enter. He performs an important **ritual.** The soul's heart is weighed on a scale against a special feather. The feather belongs to the goddess Ma'at. She's the goddess of truth and justice.

If the soul's heart is lighter than the feather, that soul can enter the underworld. Anubis protects these souls and makes sure their bodies are buried properly. They live on for **eternity**.

But if the soul's heart is heavier than the feather, the goddess Ammit will devour it.

Ammit is part crocodile, part hippopotamus, and part lion. Once she eats the heart, she destroys that person's soul.

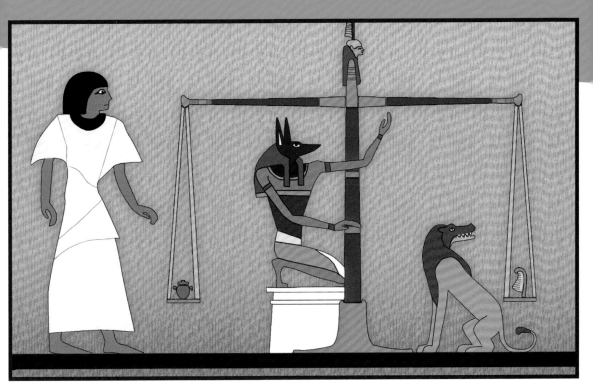

Anubis weighed a person's heart on a special scale to decide if their soul could enter the underworld.

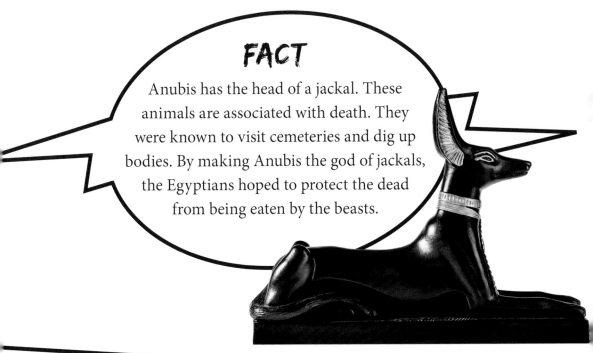

FACT

Anubis has the head of a jackal. These animals are associated with death. They were known to visit cemeteries and dig up bodies. By making Anubis the god of jackals, the Egyptians hoped to protect the dead from being eaten by the beasts.

What are Hades' other qualities? First, he's not as dramatic as the other Greek gods. He's more easygoing. For example, Athena punishes those who don't honor her. But Hades doesn't do that. He's never the villain in any Greek myth, and he doesn't get involved in messy fights.

Hades is a fair god. He doesn't take revenge on mortals for their behavior. Loyalty is also one of Hades' strengths. While some gods try to defeat Zeus, Hades never does. He respects his brother's position and keeps his focus on the underworld.

FACT

Hades is the god of the dead. But he shouldn't be confused with the god of death itself. Thanatos is the Greek god of death. He visits all souls once they die and brings them to Hades.

Hades is always honest with his wife, Persephone. He can also be a fierce warrior. He fought with the other Olympian gods in the war against the Titans.

Hades with Persephone and the three-headed dog Cerberus

What are Anubis's other duties? Many things! He takes care of funerals and protects cemeteries. His job is to make sure everyone respects the dead.

Anubis was also the inventor of **embalming** and **mummification.** This process helped preserve and protect the bodies of the dead for as long as possible. The ancient Egyptians believed it prepared dead souls for a smooth journey into the afterlife. The process also helped prevent animals from feasting on the body.

Anubis guided and protected the souls of the dead.

Pharaohs and other royalty were usually mummified. The mummies were placed in **tombs**. Anubis's job was to protect their souls. Statues of Anubis were placed in the tomb with the mummy. And prayers to him were carved into the tomb walls.

Making a Mummy

To mummify a dead body, the Egyptians began by removing all the organs, blood, and other fluids. The body was next covered with special salts to dry it out. The Egyptians then wrapped the body in strips of soft cloth and soaked it in special oils to preserve the skin. Finally, the mummy was placed in a stone coffin called a **sarcophagus**.

Hades' most useful power is the ability to become invisible. He owns a special helmet called the "Cap of Invisibility." When he wears it, he can go anywhere and do anything without being seen. The Cyclops made it for him after the war against the Titans.

The helmet makes Hades popular with other gods and goddesses. For example, Athena used it when she fought Ares in the Trojan War. Perseus also used it to escape after he killed the monstrous Medusa.

After the war against the Titans, some say Hades' helmet became even more powerful. It was said that anyone who wore the helmet could control the dead in the underworld.

FACT

Hades makes an appearance in many movies, TV shows, and books. For example, he's featured in the shows *Hercules: The Legendary Journeys* and *Xena: Warrior Princess*. He also stars in Rick Riordan's book series Percy Jackson and the Olympians.

In some Greek myths, the hero Perseus received the Cap of Invisibility from some nymphs before facing Medusa.

Anubis is lord of the dead in the afterlife. But he has another great power—shapeshifting. For example, in one myth, he turned into a lizard.

Anubis can also curse those who disturb the dead. Many tombs contain his statue as protection. It scared off grave robbers who believed they'd be cursed by disturbing the tomb.

When King Tut's tomb was discovered, several people who entered it later died. Their deaths often happened under mysterious circumstances. Some believed it was because of Anubis's curse!

King Tut's tomb was filled with many artifacts and treasures.

Anubis also performed black magic. He could communicate with the dead. Egyptian priests prayed to Anubis so they could talk with the dead too. They even wore jackal masks to call upon Anubis's powers as they mummified dead bodies.

Archaeologist Howard Carter led a team to find King Tut's tomb in 1922.

FACT

Anubis has also appeared in various movies, TV shows, and video games. He played a role in The Mummy movie series and in the show *Mr. Peabody & Sherman*.

Hades and Anubis do have one superpower in common. They're both **immortal** and will never die.

They also both hold the power of **abundance**. For example, Hades is known as the god of hidden wealth. He owns everything buried under the ground, including precious metals, minerals, and gems. Hades is also a god of **fertility** of the earth, including the vegetables and fruits that grow from it.

FACT

For ancient Egyptians, black was also the color of death and the **decay** of the body. Since Anubis is the god of death, it makes sense that his skin is black.

Anubis is connected to fertility too. His black skin symbolizes the decay of dead bodies. But it also represents the fertile earth of the Nile River Valley that grows abundant food.

The land next to the Nile River is rich and fertile for farming.

GODLY FLAWS

Both Hades and Anubis are powerful, but they aren't perfect. For example, Hades can be pretty selfish. He fell in love with Persephone but didn't have permission to marry her.

Did that stop him? Nope! He basically kidnapped her instead. He swooped down in his black chariot and snatched her away. Then he carried her off to the underworld to live there with him.

Hades kidnapped Persephone and forced her to marry him.

Persephone's mother, Demeter, searched everywhere for her daughter. She was so upset that she cursed the ground. Nothing would grow. The gods began to worry that humanity would be wiped out. Zeus commanded Hades to release Persephone.

Hades agreed, but only if Persephone didn't eat any food from the underworld. However, Hades tricked her into eating a few pomegranate seeds. Because of that, she could not leave.

Seasons of Grief and Joy

Zeus made a compromise with Hades. He agreed to let Hades keep Persephone in the underworld for part of the year. But he had to let her return to Earth for the rest of the year. When Persephone is in the underworld, her mother grieves so deeply that the harvest ends with fall and winter. When Demeter is reunited with her daughter, her joy brings new growth in spring and summer.

Persephone and Demeter

Don't get on Anubis's bad side! He has a nasty temper. In one story, a wicked god named Set disguised himself as a leopard. He was trying to steal the body of Osiris. When Anubis caught him, he burned Set all over with a hot iron. The story says that this is how the leopard got its spots. Anubis can be cruel too. He continued torturing Set and even wore Set's skin as a warning to others.

Anubis is powerful, but he has limits. This is shown in a famous tale about Anubis and his brother Bata. Anubis believed that Bata was trying to steal his wife. He tried to kill Bata in revenge, but the other gods wouldn't allow it.

Both Hades and Anubis have many strengths, powers, and flaws. With everything you now know about them, who do you think is the greater god?

Egyptian myths say that Anubis created the leopard's spots with a hot iron.

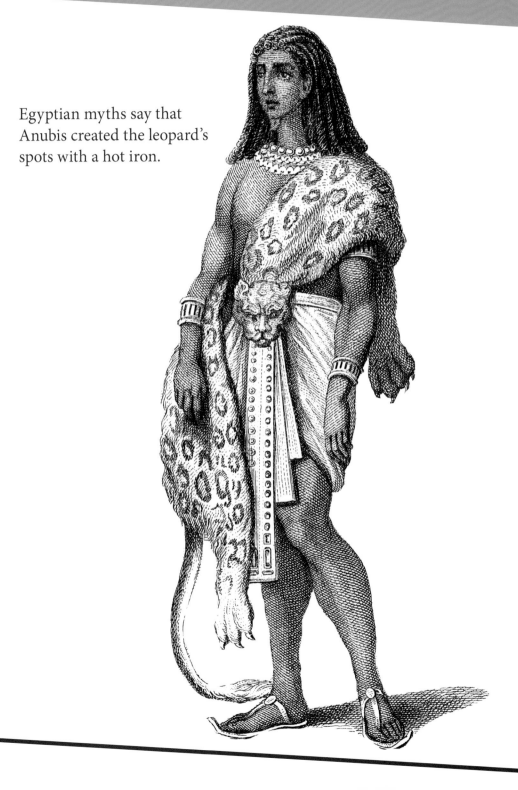

HADES VS. ANUBIS AT A GLANCE

Name: Hades

God of: The dead, wealth, and fertility, king of the underworld

Appearance: Mature man with long, dark beard and curly hair, tall, royal looking, rarely smiles

Weapon: A bident (a two-pronged weapon that looks like a pitchfork)

Strengths: Confident, commanding, fair, empathetic, easygoing, not vengeful, honest, loyal, fierce warrior

Powers and abilities: Cap of Invisibility, power over souls in the underworld, power of fertility, abundance, and the riches in the earth, immortal

Weaknesses: Selfish, sneaky, gloomy

Symbols: The three headed dog Cerberus, the key to the underworld, pomegranates

Name:	Anubis
God of:	The dead and the underworld, represents fertility of the earth
Appearance:	Has the body of a man and the head of a black jackal (a dog with pointed ears)
Weapon:	A scepter
Strengths:	Commanding, stands for justice, takes care of funerals, protects the dead and cemeteries, invented embalming and mummification
Powers and abilities:	Shapeshifting, curses those who disturb the dead or their tombs, performs black magic, can communicate with the dead, immortal, connected to fertility
Weaknesses:	Nasty temper, cruel, powers are limited
Symbols:	Scepter, mummy, jackals

GLOSSARY

abundance (uh-BUN-duhnss)—having plenty of something

embalming (im-BALM-ing)—the process of preserving a dead body so it does not decay

eternity (ih-TUR-ni-tee)—neverending time

fertility (fer-TIL-ih-tee)—the ability for a person to have a child; the ability of the land to grow crops

immortal (i-MOR-tuhl)—able to live forever

mummification (muh-mi-fuh-KAY-shuhn)—the process of drying out and preserving a dead body to create a mummy

oracle (OR-uh-kuhl)—a person who communicates with the gods and can see the future

pharaoh (FAIR-oh)—a king of ancient Egypt

ritual (RICH-oo-uhl)—a ceremony involving certain religious words and actions that are performed in a specific way

sarcophagus (sar-KAH-fuh-guhs)—a stone coffin; ancient Egyptians placed inner coffins into a sarcophagus

Titans (TYE-tuhns)—the race of powerful giants in Greek myths that existed before the Olympians

tomb (TOOM)—a room or building that holds a dead body

READ MORE

Braun, Eric. *Egyptian Myths*. North Mankato, MN: Capstone Press, 2019.

Loh-Hagan, Virginia. *Anubis*. Ann Arbor, MI: Cherry Lake Publishing, 2019.

Temple, Teri. *Hades: God of the Underworld*. Mankato, MN: Childs World, 2019.

INTERNET SITES

Anubis
kids.britannica.com/students/article/Anubis/309881

Greek Gods
historyforkids.net/ancient-greek-gods.html

Hades, God of the Underworld
greece.mrdonn.org/greekgods/hades.html

INDEX

ABOUT THE AUTHOR

Lydia Lukidis is passionate about science, the ocean, and mythology. She's the author of more than 50 trade and educational books, as well as 31 ebooks. She loves writing STEM titles, such as *Deep, Deep, Down: The Secret Underwater Poetry of the Mariana Trench* (Capstone, 2023) and *The Broken Bees' Nest* (Kane Press, 2019), which was nominated for a Cybils Award. Lydia also helps foster children's literacy and offers writing workshops and author visits in elementary schools.